P9-BZU-760

KILLER CATS
JAGUARS

By Grace Vail

Gareth Stevens
Publishing

Please visit our website, www.garethstevens.com. For a free color catalog of all our high-quality books, call toll free 1-800-542-2595 or fax 1-877-542-2596.

Library of Congress Cataloging-in-Publication Data

Vail, Grace.
Jaguars / Grace Vail.
    p. cm. — (Killer cats)
Includes index.
ISBN 978-1-4339-7004-7 (pbk.)
ISBN 978-1-4339-7005-4 (6-pack)
ISBN 978-1-4339-7003-0 (library binding)
1. Jaguar—Juvenile literature. I. Title.
QL737.C23V35 2012
599.75'5—dc23

2011043884

First Edition

Published in 2013 by
Gareth Stevens Publishing
111 East 14th Street, Suite 349
New York, NY 10003

Copyright © 2013 Gareth Stevens Publishing

Designer: Daniel Hosek
Editor: Therese Shea

Photo credits: Cover, p. 1 Peter Lilja/Stone/Getty Images; all backgrounds, pp. 5, 7, 9, 11, 15, 21
Shutterstock.com; pp. 10, 19 Thinkstock.com; p. 13 Steve Winter/National Geographic/Getty Images;
p. 17 AFP/Getty Images.

Printed in the United States of America

CPSIA compliance information: Batch #CS12GS: For further information contact Gareth Stevens, New York, New York at 1-800-542-2595.

Contents

Boldface words appear in the glossary.

Dangerous Name

The word "jaguar" comes from the Native American word *yaguara*, which means "animal that kills with a single leap." Even this wild cat's name sounds dangerous!

Jaguars are found in the largest numbers in South America. However, a few live in Central America and southern North America. Jaguars are the largest of the big cats in the Americas. They're one of four big cats in the animal group *Panthera*, which also includes lions, tigers, and leopards.

THAT'S WILD!

Members of *Panthera* are the only big cats that roar.

Of all big cats, only lions and tigers are larger than jaguars.

A Spotted Coat

A jaguar can be 6 feet (1.8 m) long and weigh more than 250 pounds (114 kg). That's the size and weight of a large person. A jaguar's tail may add another 36 inches (91 cm) onto its length.

Jaguars have black spots on their coat that form circles called "rosettes." Jaguars and leopards both have rosettes. However, some of a jaguar's rosettes have spots inside them and their outlines are "broken." A leopard's rosettes don't have spots inside.

THAT'S WILD!

If you look closely, even black jaguars have rosettes.

Jaguars can be many colors from reddish to black, though most are tan or yellow.

Jaguar Territories

Jaguars live in many kinds of **habitats**, including rainforests, grasslands, swamps, and deserts. They like to live alone in large **territories**. Male jaguars have a larger territory than female jaguars do.

Though a male may share his hunting land with females, he never shares with other males. To tell other cats to stay away, jaguars scratch trees or leave their waste in different places in their territory. By keeping other males away, the jaguar has many female **mates** to choose from.

Female jaguars are usually a bit smaller than males.

They'll Eat Anything!

Scientists have counted more than 85 animal **species** that are eaten by jaguars, including deer, **capybaras**, snakes, **tapirs**, monkeys, wild pigs, frogs, and fish. Jaguars have powerful jaws and sharp teeth that allow them to bite through the hard shells of turtles and the skulls of other **prey**.

Scientists think that it's hard for many animals to see jaguars until it's too late. A jaguar's spotted coat blends in with shadows, hiding it well.

THAT'S WILD!

Black jaguars are sometimes called black panthers. However, there are no animals named panthers.

Jaguars like to stay hidden from their prey until they're ready to attack.

Night Hunters

Jaguars hunt at night. Like other cats, they have excellent eyesight. In fact, jaguars have better eyesight in low light than in bright sunlight. Their eyes **reflect** a small amount of light so they can see better in the dark. This reflecting creates a glow called "eyeshine."

Jaguars don't usually chase their prey. Instead, they quietly follow them and kill them with a single bite. Jaguars may also climb trees and leap on prey from above.

You may see eyeshine from a house cat's eyes, too.

Water Cats

Most cats don't like to be in water, but jaguars love it! They're great swimmers and often bathe and even play in lakes and rivers. Water is also a great place for jaguars to find a meal. They eat fish as well as an alligator-like animal called a caiman.

People have seen jaguars "fishing" with their tail. They wave it over the water to attract fish looking for a meal. When a jaguar sees a fish, it scoops it out of the water with its paw.

Jaguars make dens in caves and even old buildings. However, they stay near water at all times.

15

Jaguar Cubs

After jaguars mate, the female has her cubs about 3 months later. A mother jaguar may have as many as four cubs at one time. Jaguar cubs are blind at birth and often weigh less than 2 pounds (0.9 kg). The mother takes care of them alone. She **protects** them—even from their father—until they can protect themselves.

Young jaguars stay with their mother for about 2 years. Jaguar cubs are fully grown by the time they're 4 years old.

THAT'S WILD!

Jaguars live 12 to 15 years in the wild. They can live to be 20 years old in zoos.

This jaguar mother licks her cub to keep it clean.

17

In Danger?

Other wild animals don't hunt jaguars, so they have no one to fear—except people. People have hunted jaguars for years for their beautiful coats. Jaguars are also killed by farmers and ranchers who want to keep their animals from being a jaguar's dinner.

Other threats come from people using jaguar habitats for logging and farming. Smaller habitats mean fewer animals for jaguars to hunt. Less land also means fewer mates for jaguars and fewer jaguar cubs.

THAT'S WILD!

One ancient story says that the jaguar got its spots by dipping its paws in mud and putting the mud on its body.

There are laws against killing jaguars for their fur. Unfortunately, many people break these laws.

19

Unknown Numbers

No one knows how many jaguars are still roaming the wild. Jaguars that live in thick rainforests are hard to count. However, jaguars have been labeled **endangered** in several countries, including the United States.

Scientists hope that cameras in jaguar habitats will help them learn more about this species. Hopefully, new laws and a better understanding of these big cats will cause their numbers to begin increasing once again.

JAGUARS AND LEOPARDS
Spot the Differences

Jaguar

- "broken" rosettes with spots inside
- tail is up to 36 inches (91 cm) long
- weighs up to 250 pounds (114 kg)

- *Panthera*
- rosettes on coat

Leopard

- rosettes without spots inside
- tail is up to 54 inches (137 cm) long
- weighs up to 175 pounds (79 kg)

Glossary

capybara: a large rodent that lives along rivers in Central and South America

endangered: in danger of dying out

habitat: an area where plants, animals, and other living things live

mate: one of two animals that come together to make babies. Also, to come together to make babies.

prey: an animal that is hunted by other animals for food

protect: to guard

reflect: to throw back light, heat, or sound

species: a group of animals that are all of the same kind

tapir: a hoofed animal with short legs and a large snout that lives in the forests of Central and South America and Southeast Asia

territory: an area of land that an animal lives in and guards

For More Information

BOOKS

Feinstein, Stephen. *The Jaguar: Help Save This Endangered Species!* Berkeley Heights, NJ: MyReportLinks.com Books, 2008.

Tourville, Amanda Doering. *A Jaguar Grows Up.* Minneapolis, MN: Picture Window Books, 2007.

Walker, Sally M. *Jaguars.* Minneapolis, MN: Lerner Publications, 2009.

WEBSITES

Jaguar
animals.nationalgeographic.com/animals/mammals/jaguar/
Read more about these big cats and hear what they sound like.

Mammals: Jaguar
www.sandiegozoo.org/animalbytes/t-jaguar.html
See photos of different jaguars, including a black jaguar.

Index